Cornerstones of Freedom

D-Day

R. Conrad Stein

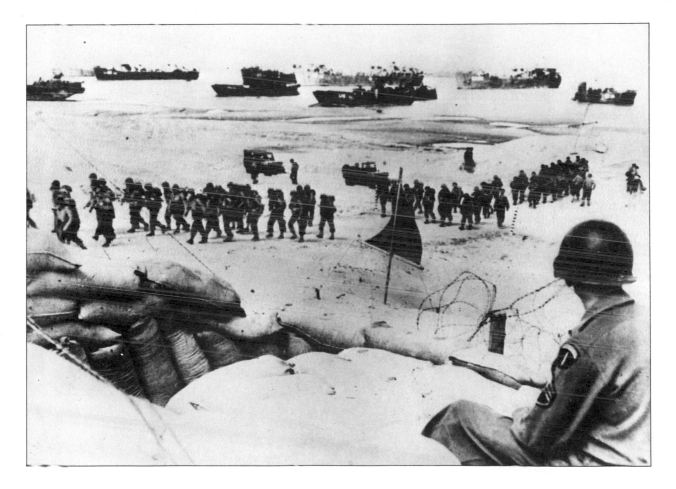

CHILDRENS PRESS ®

CHICAGO

63848

Library of Congress Cataloging-in-Publication Data

Stein, R. Conrad.
  D-Day / by R. Conrad Stein.
    p. cm. — (Cornerstones of freedom)
  Rev. ed. of: The story of D-Day. c 1977.
  Summary: Describes the events of the Allied landing on
the beaches of Normandy on June 6, 1944, the largest
invasion ever attempted in history.
  ISBN 0-516-06661-7
  1. World War, 1939-1945—Campaigns—France—
Normandy—Juvenile literature. 2. Normandy
(France)—History—Juvenile literature.
  [1. World War, 1939-1945—Campaigns—France—
Normandy. 2. Normandy (France)—History.] I. Stein,
R. Conrad. Story of D-Day. II. Title. III. Series.
D756.5.N6S73 1993   92-36809
940.54'2142—dc20   CIP
                                                AC

The engines of large aircraft roared above the town of Caen, France, on the night of June 5, 1944. Europe was in the midst of World War II. German forces had taken over most of Europe, including France. The people of Caen thought another group of bombers was passing over their town. One man, a veteran of the French army, looked up at the planes in the moonlit night. He saw a line of six two-engined planes, each one followed closely by six peculiar-looking aircraft that had no propellers. As two of the planes came nearer, the man thought he saw a cable connecting one of the two-engined planes to one of the propellerless planes. "Those aren't bombers," the Frenchmen thought to himself. "They're gliders."

The planes and the gliders rumbled over Caen and disappeared into the night. Thirty men and hundreds of pounds of equipment were jammed into each glider. Their destination was a region called Normandy on the northwest coast of France. Two important bridges there were held and guarded by German troops. The Allies needed those bridges. The men in the gliders

British paratroopers preparing to leave for Normandy on D-Day

were British paratroopers who had trained for months to perform this one operation.

At a precise moment, the towing cables were released and the planes roared into the clouds while the gliders whispered down toward the earth. Looking like huge black eagles, the gliders swooped down toward the two bridges, which could just barely be seen in the light of the full moon. As their crafts inched toward the ground, the glider pilots tried to pick out smooth areas where they could land gently, yet still close to the bridges.

One pilot thought he had found a good spot in a cornfield near the river. He eased his craft down and waited, hoping for a soft landing. With a crash and a jerk, the undercarriage of the glider hit the cornfield and bounced upward. The glider hit the ground again and skidded across the field as if it were plowing a fresh row of corn. Finally, the glider came to the end of its long skid and settled in the dirt of the cornfield. There was a second of almost churchlike silence.

"All right, lads, let's go," said an officer.

The men clambered out of the glider and rushed the bridge. The rattle of a machine gun broke the silence. Then, grenades exploded, and

A glider that crash-landed in a French field on D-Day

hundreds of tracer bullets with bright red trails streaked into the night. The Germans defending the bridges were shocked by the surprise attack, and the well-trained British paratroopers pressed toward their objective. The British overwhelmed German foxholes, one after another, with grenades, rifle fire, and bayonets. Soon paratroopers charged over the bridge and attacked German positions on the far side of the river.

In only fifteen minutes, the first battle of D-Day was over. The bridge had been captured and the British were rounding up German prisoners. One young paratrooper felt strangely disappointed. He had practiced this operation for months, and now that it was all over, it seemed to have been ridiculously easy.

Captured German soldiers trudge down a Normandy beach on D-Day.

Allied landing craft head through a choppy sea toward the Normandy coast during the early hours of the invasion.

Other battles fought during this first day of the huge Allied invasion of Europe would not be so easy.

In England, American general Dwight D. Eisenhower paced the floor of the house trailer he used as an office. Hours earlier, he had wrestled with the idea of postponing the invasion. A storm raged at sea, and the thousands of troops jammed in the flat-bottomed landing boats were bouncing about in the waters off France, most of them hopelessly seasick. A new weather front moving in from the south promised calm seas for the sixth of June, but

General Eisenhower gives a pep talk to paratroopers before they leave for Normandy on the night of June 5.

German field marshal Erwin Rommel

after that, the weather would deteriorate again. Eisenhower would have but one day to launch the most massive invasion attempt in history.

If the invasion were postponed, it would be almost a full month before there would again be enough moonlight for the airborne troops. The thousands of men assembled for D-Day could not be cooped up that long, and the American general feared someone would talk and the Germans would learn of the coming invasion. "I don't like it," he told a group of officers on the afternoon of June 5, "I don't like it, but we're stuck with it. D-Day will be the sixth of June."

In a small town in Germany, far away from the invasion beaches, Field Marshal Erwin Rommel drank coffee in his home. More than a year earlier, German dictator Adolf Hitler had chosen Rommel to construct defenses in France and command the German troops who would oppose an Allied invasion of Europe. Rommel was a hero in Germany, and was respected by all of the Allied generals. At the start of the war, he earned the nickname "Desert Fox" by skillfully maneuvering his tank divisions in North Africa to win battle after battle against the British. By 1944, however, Rommel and the German armies were on the defensive. Allied forces in Italy were steadily pushing the Germans backward, and in the east, the mighty Russian army rolled toward the German border.

German dictator Adolf Hitler

8

Expecting an Allied invasion, Rommel built a massive defense system along the Normandy coast that included obstacles embedded in the water (left) and huge concrete bunkers on the beaches (right).

Rommel knew he could expect an Allied invasion any day in northern France. For months, he had feverishly supervised the construction of enormous concrete bunkers that were armed with artillery and machine guns. Miles and miles of barbed wire were strung out on the beaches. Mines were buried in the sand, and steel posts designed to rip open the bottoms of landing boats were embedded in the sand just below the water level.

The field marshal hoped to turn the shoreline of northern Europe into one vast fortress that the Allies would never dare invade. But there were many miles of beaches, and not enough time.

The Allied plan to penetrate Rommel's "Atlantic Wall" on D-Day

The great "Atlantic Wall" Rommel hoped to create was strong in some places, but weak in others. And Rommel had no idea when or where the Allies would strike.

For the moment, Rommel felt at peace and was enjoying his vacation at home. Weather reports told him that a storm was lashing the beaches on both sides of the English Channel, and he was sure the Allies would never land in such conditions. Besides, June 6 was his wife's birthday, and he wanted to spend the day with his family.

At midnight, June 5, airplanes flying low and fast raced over the beaches at Normandy. In the darkness, German antiaircraft gunners thought they were fighters. Searchlights flicked on and German guns poured shell after shell at the formation. The planes weaved between the shell bursts and tried to dodge the long fingers of searchlight beams.

A watchful German soldier stands by a big naval gun in the Atlantic Wall.

The aircraft the Germans were firing at were Dakota transport planes, each of them packed with paratroopers. These first American paratroopers to drop on France were a small group of specially trained volunteers called "pathfinders." They were to land, move into predetermined positions, and mark drop zones with lights and flares. They would be followed by thousands of paratroopers from the 82nd and 101st Airborne divisions.

The carefully thought-out Allied invasion plans ran into difficulties from the beginning. The unexpectedly heavy antiaircraft barrage forced many of the Dakota transports off course. Of the 120 pathfinders who jumped during the early hours of June 6, fewer than 40 landed near their targets. The others were scattered over the French countryside—many miles away from their appointed areas.

It did not take long for one veteran pathfinder to realize he had been dropped at the wrong spot. He crouched in a ditch, studying his map with a small penlight. None of the terrain around him looked remotely like what was shown on the map. He snapped off his penlight and folded up his map. The flares he carried, which were supposed to mark a drop zone, were useless now. He thought about his paratrooper comrades who would be jumping within an hour. "Those poor guys," he whispered to himself. "They're going to have to come in blind."

The roar of a huge formation of airplanes flying over the English Channel was deafening. Even veteran German soldiers held their hands over their ears to protect their eardrums. Nearly nine hundred planes raced over Normandy; they were about to drop thirteen thousand paratroopers in what would be the largest airborne assault ever attempted.

These American paratroopers, crowded inside a transport plane flying over the English Channel, were about to be dropped inland, behind the main landing beaches.

The paratroopers were to land in a long narrow area behind the main landing beaches. There they would dig in and try to prevent German counterattacks on the main forces that would hit the beaches at sunrise. As the planes moved toward the landing zones, paratroop commanders searched the ground for signals from their pathfinders. Finding no signals, the commanders relied on their navigation and gave the order to jump.

Looking like falling sticks, men tumbled out of the hundreds of airplanes. When their parachutes opened, the thousands of men looked like the contents of a bag of confetti that had been emptied from a roof. After the roar of planes faded away, many of the men floating to earth thought they heard the distant chiming of church bells. For some it would be the last sound they would ever hear.

Most of the paratroopers dropped safely to the ground in flat fields. Many landed with their chutes hung up on trees and had to cut themselves down. Others landed in swamps created by Rommel, who had flooded fields to prevent airborne attack. Those who could not free themselves from their hundred-pound packs drowned, sometimes in water less than two feet deep. At least one planeload of paratroopers jumped directly into the North Atlantic, where all disappeared in the black water.

An overhead view of Allied paratroopers dropping by parachute into France

Paratroopers carrying assault equipment move along a road in northern France shortly after their drop from the sky.

There were other tragic errors committed during the early-morning hours of D-Day. A fire raged in a house in the Normandy village of Sainte-Mère-Eglise. The bell of the tall church that stood in the village square chimed wildly to summon firefighters. Townspeople formed a bucket brigade and passed water from a well to the burning house. The people of the village worked under the watchful eyes of German soldiers.

Suddenly, a German soldier shouted, *"Fallschirmjäger! Fallschirmjäger!"* ("Paratroopers! Paratroopers!") Everyone looked toward the sky, bright from the light of the burning house. Dozens of men, dangling from parachutes, were floating helplessly into the town. Those airborne soldiers were supposed to have dropped into a field south of the town, but pilot error and high winds had thrown them off course. The Germans opened fire with machine guns and rifles. Many Americans were killed before their feet ever touched French soil. Others crashed into houses or into the square itself, where they were either killed or taken prisoner.

General Eisenhower sat anxiously in his office. Initial reports from the airborne divisions told of confusion and heavy casualties. What would happen at sunrise, he thought, when the main invasion forces hit the beach?

Five hundred miles away from Normandy, Field Marshal Rommel slept soundly. German officers at the front heard word of an airborne assault, but the reports were sketchy and communication was difficult. The French underground (French people who worked secretly against the German occupation) had been cutting telephone wires again, and the airways were being jammed by American transmissions. One high-ranking German officer assumed that the reports of parachute landings at Normandy meant merely that crew members of a bomber had bailed out of a damaged plane. Besides, the German officer thought, the landing of a few paratroopers was no reason to disturb General Rommel on his vacation.

This British submarine was used as a guidepost during the invasion.

It was still dark at 5:00 A.M. when a midget submarine splashed to the surface in the waters a mile from a beach at Normandy. The submarine crew numbered only five men, but the sub was so small that each crew member felt cramped. This British submarine, the X-20, had been hiding below the surface for two days. Twenty miles away, another midget submarine, the X-23, also popped to the surface. These two subs marked the boundaries of the British and Canadian beaches. On D-Day morning, they would float in the water like goal posts on a football field, guides for hundreds of landing craft carrying thousands of soldiers.

The five crew members of the X-20 climbed to the deck of their tiny craft and began erecting a mast. On top of the mast, they would later attach a flashing green light and a large yellow flag. These markers could be seen for miles, and would guide the Allied landing craft to the correct beach. But, as every crew member knew, they would also make perfect targets for German artillery.

Behind the two midget subs was the most incredible armada ever assembled. Battleships, cruisers, destroyers, and frigates eased toward Normandy. Landing craft of every size and description tossed about in the choppy seas like toy boats in a bathtub. Not even Allied commanders knew exactly how many ships were

A landing craft crammed with troops heads for the Normandy shore.

assembled for D-Day, but the closest guess was four thousand. There were enough sailors manning boats and soldiers waiting to land to populate a small city.

The sea was calmer now, but the flat-bottomed landing craft still bounced with every wave. Seasickness from the night before had caused even the strongest men to cry without shame. Decks were slick with vomit, and during the night, some of the men had felt so miserable that they had to be held back from jumping overboard. Many of the soldiers packed into landing craft did not care how many machine guns the Germans had on the beaches. They wanted only to put their feet on solid ground.

A wide range of expressions can be seen on the faces of these Canadian troops who are just minutes away from hitting the beach.

A German soldier on guard duty along the Normandy coast watches for signs of an Allied invasion.

Most of the German soldiers on the Normandy beaches were asleep in their bunkers as the sun inched upward. One young German soldier on watch yawned and looked out to sea. As on most mornings, a fog obscured his view of the horizon. He looked back to land and, like all soldiers standing guard duty, was soon lost in a daydream. Fifteen minutes passed, and the German looked out to sea again. He could scarcely believe what he saw. Dotting the water were ships and guns that all seemed to be pointing directly at him. He tried to count them, but it seemed that with every passing second, another dozen warships popped out of the fog. This was the invasion. He was sure of it. The Allies would strike this morning.

This aerial view shows some of the four thousand Allied ships that took part in the D-Day operation.

There was a thunderous roar as the big ships opened fire. Huge battleship guns fired fourteen-inch shells. Smaller shells barked out of the destroyers. German troops hiding in concrete bunkers pressed their hands over their ears and felt themselves bouncing about as if the entire earth were shaking. When the shelling lifted, German soldiers heard the roar of airplane engines and braced themselves for a bombing attack.

Planes dropping bombs covered the sky like a steel umbrella. Young Allied troops watching the bombardment from landing craft were certain that no one could live through this holocaust. It seemed as if the entire beach were exploding. But the veterans knew better. There would still be plenty of Germans left when they landed.

Long lines of assault craft churned toward shore. Each one of the American, British, Canadian, and Free French soldiers crowded into the boats felt alone with his fears. Would the beaches be mined? Would the Germans use poison gas?

Boats carrying American soldiers of the Twenty-ninth Division moved toward a beach that had the code name "Omaha." Peering over the tops of the ramps, the soldiers saw Rommel's handiwork. Concrete and steel posts jutted from the sand of the beach. The tops of the posts were mined, and barbed wire was strung between them. The beach looked like a steel jungle.

Tanks, guns, and other armored vehicles churn toward the shore.

A landing craft limps along after being hit by German coastal guns.

A soldier whose landing craft was blown apart by a German sea mine is rescued by a Coast Guard barge.

The clumsy landing boats bounced in the waves as they bored toward the beach. Four hundred yards to go, now three hundred. Where were the Germans? Would this be an easy landing? Suddenly, one of the landing craft exploded. Shattered bodies flew from it and splashed into the water. Another landing craft was hit and sank like a rock.

The German artillery pieces that were dug into the cliffs near Omaha looked directly down on the long lines of slow-moving boats. "This will be like target practice," said one German soldier.

Still the hundreds of landing boats moved forward. They bumped against the beach, ramps dropped, and men laden with heavy packs

When the landing boats came close enough to shore, their ramps dropped, and Allied infantrymen hit the beach.

splashed into water that was anywhere from three- to six-feet deep. German machine guns opened fire at the men wading through the water. History would remember this beachhead as "bloody Omaha."

On another American beach, code-named "Utah," General Theodore Roosevelt, Jr., (son of former president Teddy Roosevelt) studied a map. His men of the Fourth Division, unlike those who had landed at nearby Omaha Beach, had had only a few shots fired at them. The general looked confused as he stared at the map. Finally he called a major over to him and said, "We're on the wrong beach."

American soldiers help each other to shore at Utah Beach.

The major read the map and agreed. Smoke created by the pre-invasion bombardment must have confused the pilots of the landing boats, and the Fourth Division had hit the beach more than a mile away from their target. Thousands of troops were yet to land, and the major asked if they should land at the original site.

"Nope, our war starts right here," the general said as he pointed to the beach now held by the Fourth Division. "Now let's move inland."

General Roosevelt would later learn how fortunate he and his men were to have landed at the wrong beach. The original landing site was defended by hundreds of Germans, all well dug in and heavily armed. Had the landing party hit the correct beach, the Fourth Division would have faced the same slaughter as the men of the Twenty-ninth were experiencing at Omaha.

The second wave of landing boats pushed to the sands of Omaha Beach. The GIs charging off the landing craft could hardly believe what they saw around them. Wrecked landing boats lay strewn on the beaches. Torn and bloody bodies were everywhere. Men hid behind anti-tank obstacles set up by the enemy while the Germans rained fire at them with machine guns, artillery and mortars. New soldiers at Omaha became instant veterans as they plunged into the middle of this bloody battle.

Theodore Roosevelt, Jr.

Though the first troops to hit Omaha Beach were nearly wiped out by German fire, backup troops slowly and painfully gained ground.

American GIs buried themselves in foxholes dug into the sand at Utah Beach while waiting for orders to move inland against the Germans.

Wounded GIs rest against a cliff on Omaha Beach while waiting to be evacuated.

As the GIs pressed themselves into the sand, they were amazed to see one man calmly walking about the beach as if he were a civilian on his way to work. Colonel George Taylor of the First Infantry Division knew that courage is often born of necessity. He had put his life in the hands of fate and urged his men to do the same. The colonel walked erect, ignoring the furious enemy machine-gun fire. "Listen to me, men," he shouted above the din of battle. "There are only two kinds of men on this beach. Those who are already dead, and those who are about to die. Now let's go inland and die. Get off this damn beach."

One by one, the American GIs got to their feet and advanced to the high ground in front of them. Many were cut down by machine-gun fire and still others were blown apart by mines, but the rest continued to push forward. By dusk of D-Day, the Americans at Omaha had moved more than a mile inland. There had been twenty-five hundred casualties.

On Utah Beach, huge landing ships, their front hatches yawning open, pushed against the beach while trucks, jeeps, tanks, and guns rolled out of them. The scene reminded some of a grotesque big-city traffic jam. Ahead, the front-line troops of the Fourth Division advanced at a faster speed than anyone could have imagined.

Allied men and equipment poured ashore after Omaha Beach was secured.

An American gun battery in action on the Omaha beachhead

The lead man of a Fourth Division patrol walked cautiously up a Normandy path. So far, the GI had seen no Germans. He turned a corner near a patch of tall bushes. Suddenly, he saw another soldier and dove to the ground. The other man saw the American and also hit the dirt. But both recognized that the uniforms of the opponents were not German.

The Fourth Division GI hid behind a rock and called out, "Hey, are you airborne?"

"Yeah," the paratrooper answered. "What took you guys so long to get here?"

The midget submarines, X-20 and X-23, tore off their huge yellow flags and flashing green lights and set a course for England. They had marked the beaches for the thousands of British and Canadian soldiers who, like the Americans, were now fighting their way inland. All morning, the Germans had shelled landing craft and any other ship that came within their range. But these two tiny submarines floating in the waves just a mile off shore escaped untouched. Now they could go home. Their job on D-Day was finished.

In his office in England, General Eisenhower smiled when he was told of the linkup between the airborne forces and the Fourth Division at Utah Beach. He was sure he had a secure beachhead and wondered how soon he could go to France to congratulate his men.

It was just after ten in the morning in Germany when Field Marshal Rommel answered his

General Eisenhower (at left) smiles in France a few weeks after the invasion.

Three weeks after D-Day, these German officers emerged from their hideout at Cherbourg, France, and surrendered to American troops.

American GIs were greeted joyously when they liberated Paris on August 25.

phone. An excited German officer told him the Allies were landing a huge force at Normandy. Rommel listened quietly, and after he hung up, said, "Normandy. I should have known." D-Day was over. The largest amphibious invasion ever attempted had been a success. By nightfall, 155,000 Allied soldiers had landed at Normandy and had liberated eighty miles of French soil. In the months to come, the Allies would sweep toward Germany with such power that no one would be able to stop them.

Four months after D-Day, Field Marshal Rommel was dead. He had been forced to take poison after he participated in a plot to assassinate Adolf Hitler, the man who had

Eleven weeks after D-Day, Allied troops swept triumphantly into Paris.

The tank that remains on this Normandy beach is a permanent reminder of what happened there on June 6, 1944.

brought so much misery to Europe and the rest of the world. General Eisenhower retired from the army shortly after World War II. He later became the president of the United States.

On the Normandy beaches today, there are many plaques and markers indicating sites of individual action that took place during this historic battle. Perhaps the most bittersweet of them all is a simple wooden sign that stands near the cliffs of Pointe du Hoc, where a brief but violent battle was fought. The sign reads:

HERE THE WARRIORS SLEEP. THE CHAOS OF
BATTLE HAS UNITED THEM FOR ETERNITY.

INDEX

PHOTO CREDITS

Cover, 1, Agence France Presse; 2, UPI/Bettmann; 4, Imperial War Museum, London; 5, UPI/Bettmann; 6, 7 (bottom), U.S. Army Photograph; 7 (top), UPI/Bettmann; 8 (top), AP/Wide World; 8 (bottom), U.S. Army Photograph; 9 (top left, right), AP/Wide World; 9 (bottom left), 10, UPI/Bettmann; 11, 12, AP/Wide World; 13, 14, UPI/Bettmann; 16, 17, 18, AP/Wide World; 19, Agence France Presse; 20, 21, 22 (both photos), UPI/Bettmann; 23, Agence France Presse; 24, 25 (bottom), U.S. Army Photograph; 25 (top), AP/Wide World; 26 (top), UPI/Bettmann; 26 (bottom), U.S. Army Photograph; 27, UPI/Bettmann; 28, 29 (both photos), U.S. Army Photograph; 30 (both photos), AP/Wide World; 31, © Kenneth Rapalee/Root Resources

Picture Identifications:
Cover: The ramp of a landing craft drops, and American infantrymen wade to shore at Omaha Beach on D-Day.
Page 1: Allied troops disembark at a Normandy beachhead.
Page 2: Tow planes release gliders over Normandy during the invasion. The hedges surrounding the small Normandy fields made landings tricky, and many of the gliders crashed, as can be seen at the bottom of the photograph.

Project Editor: Shari Joffe
Designer: Karen Yops
Photo Editor: Jan Izzo
Cornerstones of Freedom Logo: David Cunningham

ABOUT THE AUTHOR

R. Conrad Stein was born and raised in Chicago. He enlisted in the Marine Corps at the age of eighteen and served for three years. He then attended the University of Illinois, where he received a bachelor's degree in history. He later studied in Mexico, earning an advanced degree from the University of Guanajuato. Mr. Stein is the author of many books, articles, and short stories for young people.

Mr. Stein lives in Chicago with his wife and their daughter Janna.